Pop Culture & Entertainment Critique: Revolution in Heels: Fashion Culture, Power, and the Politics of Beauty

How the History of Fashion, Trends, and Consumerism Shape Identity, Beauty Standards, and Fashion Empowerment

Jordan R Sloane

Contents

Fashion Is Political, Whether You Like It or Not   v

Part One
The Power of Dress – What We Wear and What It Says About Us

1. The Uniform of Power – How Clothes Signal Authority (or the Lack of It)   3
2. Beauty Standards and the Economics of Insecurity   8
3. The Fast Fashion Paradox – Affordable Expression or Ethical Disaster?   14

Part Two
Fashion as Rebellion – When Style Becomes a Statement

4. Dressing the Revolution – From Suffragettes to Riot Grrrls   21
5. The Politics of Hair – A Crown or a Constraint?   26
6. High Heels, Lipstick, and Feminism – Empowerment or Oppression?   32

Part Three
The Future of Fashion – Where Do We Go From Here?

7. The Death of Trends – Will Fashion Ever Be Truly Inclusive?   39
8. The AI Stylist and the Metaverse Closet – The Digital Future of Fashion   45
9. The Case for Wearing Whatever the Hell You Want   51

Conclusion: Fashion as a Tool, Not a Trap   57

Fashion Is Political, Whether You Like It or Not

I still remember the outfit. A perfectly tailored blazer—navy, structured, commanding—paired with sleek black trousers and a pair of pointed-toe heels that clicked against the floor with every step. It was the kind of ensemble that made me feel invincible, as if the right seams and stitches could armor me against the world. And maybe they could—until they couldn't.

Because I also remember another outfit. A dress, soft and floral, cinched at the waist. Too feminine, too delicate, too unserious. Or at least, that's what I was told. "You might want to rethink that," someone had said, their voice dripping with the kind of condescension reserved for those who think they understand the unspoken rules but really don't. The rules that dictate what we wear, how we present ourselves, and—more importantly—how we are perceived. The rules that say fashion is frivolous until it's powerful.

Let's get one thing straight: fashion has never been just about clothes. It's about identity. Power. Class. Race. Gender. It's a cultural script, a language we speak before we even open our mouths. And yet, fashion is often dismissed as something shallow, a playground of vanity and consumerism rather than a legitimate site of discourse.

Fashion Is Political, Whether You Like It or Not

The truth? Fashion is one of the most potent forces shaping our world. What we wear has dictated who gets taken seriously, who is excluded, who is feared, and who is celebrated. A hoodie can signify menace or genius. A suit can open doors—or reinforce who's not allowed inside. A headscarf can be an emblem of faith, a target of discrimination, or a radical reclamation of identity.

Throughout history, clothing has been both a weapon and a shield. Suffragettes marched for their rights in crisp white dresses, deliberately rejecting the caricature of the hysterical woman. Black Panthers donned leather jackets and berets as a visual declaration of strength and defiance. Punk rockers slashed and safety-pinned their clothes as a middle finger to the establishment. From corsets to combat boots, our choices in dress have been policed, politicized, and profoundly influential.

But fashion's power doesn't stop at symbolism—it has an economic grip on our lives. The global fashion industry is worth trillions, fueling endless cycles of trends that demand we keep up, buy more, and never quite feel enough. The beauty industry thrives on manufactured insecurities, selling us the illusion of effortless perfection while ensuring it remains just out of reach. And in the age of social media, personal style has become public currency, shaping careers, identities, and perceptions with every carefully curated post.

This book is about the intersection of fashion, beauty, and power—how what we wear shapes who we are and how the world treats us. It's about the ways fashion can liberate and constrain, how trends are born out of rebellion and then sold back to us as conformity. It's about the economic, social, and political undercurrents embedded in every stitch, shade of lipstick, and sneaker drop.

Throughout these pages, we'll dissect the coded language of clothing, the economics of insecurity, and the ways style can be both an act of resistance and a tool of oppression. We'll examine fashion's role in movements, from feminism to racial justice, and unpack the contradictions of an industry that sells empowerment while profiting off self-doubt.

Fashion Is Political, Whether You Like It or Not

Most importantly, this book is a call to reclaim fashion on our own terms. To understand it. To critique it. To use it wisely. Because whether we like it or not, fashion is political. And the sooner we acknowledge its power, the better we can harness it.

Part One
The Power of Dress – What We Wear and What It Says About Us

The Uniform of Power – How Clothes Signal Authority (or the Lack of It)

The Clothes Make the (Wo)Man—Or Do They?

Imagine walking into a boardroom. Around the table, you see a sea of navy and charcoal suits—crisp, pressed, and practically humming with authority. Now, imagine someone striding in wearing ripped jeans, a leather jacket, and sneakers. One of two things is happening here: either they're about to be laughed out of the room, or they own the damn company.

Clothing isn't just fabric draped over our bodies; it's coded language. A silent social contract. We are constantly reading each other based on what we wear, drawing conclusions—conscious or not—about competence, wealth, and worth. It's why politicians fine-tune their outfits like PR statements, why CEOs and startup founders have signature "uniforms" (whether it's Zuckerberg's gray T-shirt or Anna Wintour's ever-present sunglasses), and why women in power still face a balancing act between looking authoritative and being deemed "likable" enough.

Fashion signals status, identity, and belonging—but it can also mark someone as an outsider. Throughout history, marginalized groups have used clothing as resistance, while those in power have used it to enforce hierarchy. A hoodie can be an emblem of streetwear culture—or a death sentence, as in the case of Trayvon Martin. A suit can open doors, but only if you're the "right" kind of person wearing it.

In this chapter, we'll explore how different styles communicate authority (or the lack of it), the gendered politics of power dressing, and the ways marginalized communities have turned fashion into a battleground for visibility and self-determination.

The Power Suit, The Little Black Dress, and the Hoodie: Fashion as a Status Symbol

Few things are as instantly recognizable as a power suit. From the Wall Street banker to the Supreme Court justice, the suit is synonymous with authority. It's a visual shorthand for control, competence, and command. The sharper the cut, the more tailored the fit, the more power it wields. But power dressing isn't just about suits—it's about knowing (and manipulating) the expectations that come with them.

Take the little black dress. Unlike the suit, which signals authority in a way that is almost militaristic, the LBD is about a different kind of power: one that's social, seductive, and carefully calibrated. A woman in an LBD is seen as sophisticated, but she's also playing within the boundaries of acceptability. Too short, and it's "unprofessional." Too modest, and it's "matronly." Women's clothing is always a negotiation—a game of threading the needle between too much and not enough.

And then there's the hoodie, the most controversial piece of clothing in modern history. It's a staple of Silicon Valley billionaires, but on a Black teenager, it can be seen as a threat. The hoodie is proof that fashion is never just about style; it's about who gets to wear what without consequence.

. . .

Dressing as Resistance: From Suffragettes' White to Black Panthers' Leather

Fashion has long been a weapon of rebellion. In the early 20th century, suffragettes wore white as a symbol of purity and righteousness—turning a traditionally feminine color into a radical statement. Decades later, the Black Panthers adopted black leather jackets, turtlenecks, and berets, creating a militant, unified aesthetic that demanded visibility and strength. Their style wasn't just about looking good; it was a carefully curated image of defiance and power.

Queer and trans communities have also used fashion to carve out space for themselves. Ballroom culture in the 1980s turned gender expression into an art form, creating new rules of beauty and self-presentation. Drag, once seen as purely performative, is now a political act in a world that still polices gender norms.

Even today, clothing remains a battleground. Hijabs, natural hair, and cultural garments are still sites of discrimination, proving that the fight over who gets to wear what—and what it means—is far from over.

The Controversy of Women's Dress Codes in Corporate and Political Spaces

Let's talk about heels. In 2016, a receptionist in London was sent home from work because she refused to wear high heels. The incident sparked outrage, but the reality is that women have been subjected to dress codes that men never have to think about for centuries.

In corporate spaces, the rules are clear but unspoken. Women must be polished but not intimidating, feminine but not frivolous, stylish but not distracting. A man can wear the same navy suit every day and be seen as consistent. A woman who repeats an outfit too often risks being called lazy or unkempt. The double standard is exhausting—and expensive.

The political arena isn't much better. Hillary Clinton's pantsuits were dissected more than her policies. Alexandria Ocasio-Cortez's red lipstick became a statement. Kamala Harris' Converse sneakers were an entire news cycle. Meanwhile, male politicians wear the same uninspired suits and ties without a second thought.

Dress codes aren't just about aesthetics—they're about control. They reinforce power structures and define who belongs in certain spaces. When women and marginalized groups push back—whether by wearing sneakers in the Senate or rocking their natural hair in the boardroom—it's not just fashion. It's resistance.

CONCLUSION: Fashion as a Tool of Power

What we wear is never neutral. Clothing is a uniform, whether we like it or not. It can grant access or deny it. It can signal authority or undermine it. And in a world where perception is reality, understanding the politics of dress isn't just about looking good—it's about knowing how the game is played.

In the end, the question isn't just *what* we wear, but *who* gets to wear it—and on whose terms. Fashion has always been a tool of power. The challenge is making sure we're the ones wielding it.

Beauty Standards and the Economics of Insecurity

The Price of Pretty

No one ever says the quiet part out loud: that beauty is a currency, and like any currency, some people are born with more of it than others. But here's the real kicker—no matter where you start on the so-called beauty hierarchy, the system is designed to keep you spending. The perfect skin, the ideal body, the effortless glow—it's all a moving target, an illusion sustained by an industry worth billions, built on the promise that if you just try *a little bit harder*, you'll finally be enough.

The truth? Looking "effortless" is anything but.

From corsets to "Instagram Face," beauty standards have never been stagnant. They evolve just fast enough to keep us on our toes, ensuring that what was desirable yesterday is outdated (or worse, embarrassing) today. This chapter unpacks how beauty myths have evolved, who profits from our insecurities, and why beauty is always political—especially when race, gender, and power come into play.

. . .

The Evolution of the Beauty Myth: From Corsets to Instagram Face

Let's start with a history lesson.

For centuries, beauty standards have shifted according to who holds power. In the Victorian era, beauty meant pale skin, cinched waists, and delicate features—an aesthetic that signaled wealth because only the rich could afford to be fragile. The working class couldn't squeeze into a corset and lounge around in lace; they were too busy, well, working.

Fast forward to the 1920s, and suddenly the ideal woman was a slim, boyish flapper, rejecting the restrictive femininity of the previous era. By the 1950s, Marilyn Monroe's curves were the gold standard. By the 1990s, heroin chic was in, and bodies were expected to be impossibly thin. Today, we're in the era of **Instagram Face**—the hyper-smooth, high-cheekboned, plumped-lipped, contoured-to-perfection look popularized by the Kardashians and reinforced by filters, fillers, and FaceTune.

Each of these beauty ideals has one thing in common: they were never *really* attainable. Not without money, time, and sometimes a fair amount of pain. The goalposts are always shifting, and that's not an accident—it's business.

The Financial Burden of Keeping Up

Beauty isn't just a look; it's an industry. And it's not just about makeup anymore. It's skincare, injectables, hair treatments, gym memberships, wellness regimens, laser facials, body sculpting, and surgical enhancements. The modern woman is expected to glow from the inside out—and that glow costs a fortune.

Let's break it down. The average woman spends:

• **$313 per month** on beauty-related expenses (which adds up to about **$225,000** over a lifetime).

• **$3,756 per year** on skincare, makeup, and hair care.

- **$1,300+ per year** on gym memberships and fitness-related expenses.
- **$400+ per session** for Botox or fillers (which require maintenance every few months).
- **$5,000–$15,000** for a single plastic surgery procedure.

And those are just the surface-level numbers. The real cost of beauty is deeper—it's the hours spent in front of the mirror, the anxiety of aging, the constant feeling that you could (and should) be doing more. It's the unspoken truth that looking youthful, thin, and conventionally attractive is still an unspoken requirement in many industries, from Hollywood to high finance.

Men, of course, have their own grooming expectations, but the pressure isn't the same. Aging for men is "distinguished." For women, it's a crisis.

Why Looking "Effortless" Is a Full-Time Job

We love the idea of the "cool girl." You know the one—the effortlessly gorgeous woman who *just wakes up looking like that*. No heavy makeup, no obvious effort, just *naturally* beautiful. The problem? It's a scam.

The "effortless" beauty ideal is built on invisible labor. That dewy, no-makeup makeup look? It requires a 10-step skincare routine, a $100 foundation that looks like skin, and a hairstylist who knows how to make "bedhead" look intentional. The "toned but not too muscular" body? That's hours in the gym, but only the right kind of workouts (pilates and yoga, not "bulky" lifting). Even the rise of the "clean girl aesthetic"—slicked-back hair, minimalist beauty, quiet luxury—is a privilege, because it assumes you have naturally symmetrical features, clear skin, and enough money to invest in *quality over quantity*.

Women are told to be low-maintenance, but also to be beautiful. To look "natural," but to never actually *be* natural. And the second you fall behind, there's another product, another treatment, another *solution* to fix you.

The Intersection of Race and Beauty Ideals—Who Gets to Set the Standard?

Here's the thing about beauty standards: they are never neutral. They have always reflected power structures, which means they have always been *racialized*.

For centuries, whiteness has been positioned as the beauty ideal. Fair skin, European features, silky straight hair—these were the markers of desirability, and anything outside that standard was considered "exotic" at best, unacceptable at worst.

This bias isn't just historical—it's still shaping the beauty industry today. Consider:

- **Skin-lightening creams** are a billion-dollar industry, with products marketed aggressively in Asia, Africa, and Latin America, reinforcing colorism and the idea that lighter skin = better.

- **Black women are disproportionately penalized for their natural hair.** Corporate dress codes, school policies, and even laws have been used to police Black hair, deeming afros, braids, and locs as "unprofessional."
- **Beauty brands historically catered to lighter skin tones.** Fenty Beauty (Rihanna's makeup line) was groundbreaking not because it was the first to acknowledge darker skin tones—but because it was one of the few to do so in a mainstream way.

Even plastic surgery trends reflect these biases. Procedures like rhinoplasty were once primarily about *Westernizing* features—thinning noses, reducing lip size, creating a more "refined" (read: Eurocentric) look. Now, the same full lips and curvier bodies that were once stigmatized are desirable—so long as they're on white women. The Kardashians have built an empire off of aesthetics historically associated with Black and Latina women, raising the question: who gets to profit from these beauty standards, and who gets punished for them?

Conclusion: Beauty as a Rigged Game

Beauty has never been just about looking good. It's about power, privilege, and control. The goal is never to *achieve* beauty—it's to *chase* it, to keep spending, keep striving, keep believing that you're just one more product away from perfection.

So what's the solution? Some argue for radical self-acceptance, but that's easier said than done in a world that still rewards beauty with social and economic advantages. Others advocate for redefining beauty altogether—celebrating diversity, dismantling Eurocentric standards, and demanding inclusivity in fashion and media.

But maybe the real rebellion is simply *opting out*—acknowledging that beauty is a game designed for us to lose and choosing, instead, to play by our own rules.

Because at the end of the day, the most dangerous thing a woman can be is someone who no longer feels like she has to fix herself.

The Fast Fashion Paradox – Affordable Expression or Ethical Disaster?

The $5 Shirt That Costs a Fortune

Somewhere in the world, right now, a fashion trend is dying.

A dress that was "must-have" last month is now marked down to clearance. A pair of jeans that once dominated Instagram feeds has been replaced by the next viral silhouette. A handbag, once aspirational, is now embarrassingly outdated.

And as trends cycle faster than ever, the demand for cheap, disposable clothing has skyrocketed. Enter **fast fashion**—the industry's biggest paradox. It democratizes style, making trendy clothes accessible to the masses. But it also fuels exploitation, environmental devastation, and a culture of mindless consumption.

Fast fashion is built on an impossible promise: that you can have it all—style, affordability, variety—without consequence. The reality? Every $5 T-shirt and $10 dress has a hidden cost. Someone, somewhere, is paying for it. The question is: *who?*

THE RISE OF ZARA, Shein, and the Speed of Trend Cycles

Not so long ago, fashion followed the **four-season model**: spring, summer, fall, winter. Designers would release collections months in advance, setting the tone for what was to come. Magazines dictated trends. Shopping was intentional, an investment.

Then, the 2000s happened.

Brands like Zara, H&M, and Forever 21 rewrote the rules, churning out new collections every few weeks instead of every few months. Suddenly, fashion wasn't about seasonal cycles—it was about **speed**. And the faster fashion moved, the faster our collective attention spans shrank.

Then came **Shein**, an ultra-fast fashion juggernaut that put the entire industry on steroids. Shein isn't just fast—it's *instantaneous*. While Zara's supply chain takes weeks, Shein can identify a microtrend, design it, produce it, and have it for sale in **days**. The result? A never-ending flood of **new, cheap, disposable fashion**, driven by social media's appetite for *more, more, more*.

Some stats to put this into perspective:

• In 2000, the average person bought **about 20 new garments per year**.

• Today, thanks to fast fashion, that number has **tripled**.

• Shein uploads **6,000+ new designs daily**—more than some brands release in a year.

• The average Zara piece takes **two weeks** from design to store shelf.

• The world produces **100 billion garments per year**—that's about **14 pieces of clothing per person on Earth**.

What happens when you make fashion **this cheap, this accessible, this endless**? People stop seeing clothes as things to keep and start treating them as disposable.

THE HIDDEN LABOR OF FASHION: Who Pays the Real Price?

Every time a Shein haul goes viral—featuring massive bags of trendy clothes purchased for the price of a Starbucks order—there's a cost that's not included in the total.

That cost is paid by the **garment workers**—mostly women, mostly underpaid, mostly in countries where labor laws are weak or nonexistent.

In 2013, the **Rana Plaza factory collapse** in Bangladesh killed over 1,100 garment workers. They had been sewing clothes for brands like Primark, Mango, and Benetton in a building so structurally unsound that workers had already reported massive cracks in the walls. The factory owners ignored them. Production deadlines mattered more than human lives.

A decade later, little has changed.

Fast fashion thrives on **cheap labor and unsafe working conditions**. Garment workers often make less than **$3 per day**, working **14+ hour shifts** in sweatshop conditions. And because companies like Shein rely on complex, outsourced supply chains, they can easily **deny responsibility** when allegations of forced labor or worker abuse surface.

The business model is simple:
1 Pay workers as little as possible.
2 Cut corners on materials.
3 Flood the market with ultra-cheap products.
4 Rinse and repeat.

Consumers get a $10 dress. Brands make billions. The workers? They barely survive.

And it's not just the workers paying the price.

The Environmental Toll: Why Your Closet Might Be Killing the Planet

Here's a not-so-fun fact: **fashion is one of the most polluting industries on the planet**.

- The fashion industry produces **10% of global carbon emissions**—more than **aviation and shipping combined**.

- It takes **2,700 liters of water** to make a single cotton T-shirt—enough for **one person to drink for 2.5 years**.
- Over **85% of all textiles** end up in landfills or incinerated each year.
- **Synthetic fabrics (like polyester)** shed microplastics every time they're washed, polluting oceans and entering our food chain.

Fast fashion accelerates **waste culture**. Because clothes are so cheap, people don't think twice about discarding them after a few wears. In the U.S. alone, **an estimated 11 million tons of textile waste** is dumped in landfills each year.

Even "donating" your clothes doesn't solve the problem. Most thrift stores can't sell the sheer volume of fast fashion they receive. Instead, these clothes are **shipped off to developing countries**, where they flood local markets, destroy domestic textile industries, and eventually end up **piling up in massive waste dumps**.

The irony? Fast fashion claims to be about "democratizing" style, but its environmental destruction disproportionately affects **the poorest communities**—the very people who have the least power in the industry.

THE INFLUENCER ECONOMY and the Pressure to Constantly "Refresh" Your Look

Social media has turned fashion into an **endless cycle of consumption**.

On TikTok, #SheinHaul has billions of views. Influencers post videos of massive clothing hauls, where they try on **dozens of outfits at once**—most of which they'll probably never wear again. Fashion is no longer just about self-expression; it's about *content creation*.

There's an **unspoken pressure** to never be seen in the same outfit twice. Outfit repeating? That's for regular people. Influencers (and even everyday users) are expected to keep **refreshing their looks**, driving demand for **cheap, disposable fashion**.

And who benefits?

Not the consumer, who is stuck in an **infinite shopping loop**.

Not the workers, who are still underpaid.

Not the planet, which is drowning in textile waste.

The only winners? The fast fashion brands making billions off **our collective insecurity**.

Is Ethical Consumerism Even Possible?

So, what's the solution? **Boycott fast fashion? Only buy sustainable brands? Thrift everything?**

The problem is, "ethical fashion" is often **expensive and inaccessible**. Not everyone can afford a $200 ethically made dress, and **secondhand shopping isn't a realistic solution when fast fashion dominates the resale market**.

The real issue isn't just individual consumption—it's **systemic overproduction**. No single person can undo the environmental and labor crisis caused by billion-dollar corporations. What's needed is **regulation, corporate accountability, and a complete shift in how fashion is produced and consumed**.

But until that happens, the best we can do is **be aware**:

• Buy less, choose well, make it last.

• Support brands that prioritize **ethics over exploitation**.

• Push for **transparency and better labor laws**.

• Challenge the culture of **hyper-consumption and trend-chasing**.

Because if we don't, fast fashion won't just keep destroying **our wallets, our planet, and garment workers' lives**—it will keep convincing us that all of this is normal.

And it's not.

Part Two
Fashion as Rebellion – When Style Becomes a Statement

Dressing the Revolution – From Suffragettes to Riot Grrrls

Fashion as a Protest Sign

In 2017, a sea of **pink pussy hats** flooded the streets in one of the largest protests in U.S. history. The Women's March wasn't just about policy—it was about **visibility**. The knitted hats, with their tongue-in-cheek feminist symbolism, were a reminder that fashion isn't just about looking good—it's about *being seen*.

But this wasn't the first time clothing became a weapon of resistance. From the **white dresses of the suffragettes** to the **leather jackets of the Black Panthers**, fashion has long been a tool of rebellion, identity, and political expression.

Throughout history, oppressed groups have **harnessed style as a statement**, flipping the script on what society expects them to wear. Whether it's a miniskirt, a safety-pinned punk jacket, or a rainbow flag draped over someone's shoulders at a Pride march, fashion has the power to say: *I exist. I resist. And you can't ignore me.*

This chapter explores how style has shaped—and been shaped by—political and social movements, proving that even the most "superficial" choices are often the most radical.

. . .

Suffragettes in White: **Dressing for the Vote**

Before social media, before viral hashtags, before protest t-shirts, the suffragettes **used fashion as their platform**.

In the early 1900s, when women were fighting for the right to vote, they knew they had to craft a public image that **commanded attention without inviting backlash**. The solution? **White dresses**, which symbolized purity, morality, and dignity—qualities their opponents insisted they lacked.

It was a strategic move. By dressing in flowing white garments, suffragettes created a striking contrast against a sea of black-suited male politicians. The choice was both **aesthetic and tactical**—photos of suffragette parades printed in newspapers stood out, making their cause impossible to ignore.

Fast forward to 2019, and U.S. congresswomen, including Alexandria Ocasio-Cortez, revived this tradition, wearing all-white to the State of the Union to protest policies restricting women's rights. Over a century later, **the uniform of resistance still worked**.

Punk, Riot Grrrls, and the Power of Dressing Like You Don't Care

If the suffragettes used fashion to be **taken seriously**, punks and Riot Grrrls used it to say: **fuck your rules**.

The punk movement of the 1970s was a full-blown rebellion against authority—politically, musically, and sartorially. Ripped fishnets, studded jackets, Doc Martens, neon mohawks—this wasn't just a look; it was a **middle finger to conformity**. If mainstream fashion was about beauty and desirability, punk was about the opposite—wearing clothes that made people uncomfortable.

In the 1990s, **Riot Grrrls**—a feminist punk movement—took this DIY aesthetic and **weaponized** it against misogyny. They scrawled **"slut" and "bitch" on their bodies**, took control of their sexuality, and used **baby-doll dresses and combat boots** to mix femininity with rage.

And it wasn't just about music—it was about **calling out sexism in culture, politics, and fashion itself**. While mainstream feminism was still debating whether miniskirts were "empowering" or "problematic," Riot Grrrls said: *wear what you want, and if it pisses people off, even better.*

Black Panthers, BLM, and the Politics of Streetwear

Few groups have used fashion as effectively as the **Black Panthers**.

In the 1960s and '70s, the Black Panther Party's **signature look—black leather jackets, berets, and sunglasses—wasn't just for aesthetics. It was an intentional, militarized uniform of resistance**.

- **Black leather** = strength, defiance, and power.
- **Berets** = unity, solidarity, and nod to revolutionary movements worldwide.
- **Sunglasses** = mystery, protection, and a refusal to be vulnerable under a racist gaze.

They dressed like revolutionaries because they *were* revolutionaries. Their fashion choices weren't just about looking cool—they were about **reclaiming Black identity** in a country that had criminalized Blackness.

Decades later, the **Black Lives Matter movement** has carried that legacy forward, though in a different way. Instead of a uniform, **BLM's style of resistance is streetwear-driven**—hoodies, sneakers, and bold graphic tees with statements like *I CAN'T BREATHE* and *STOP KILLING US*.

The hoodie itself has become **a symbol of racial injustice**, particularly after the murder of Trayvon Martin in 2012. When NBA players, celebrities, and activists started wearing hoodies in solidarity, it became clear that what Black people wear isn't just *fashion* —it's **a political statement, whether they want it to be or not**.

The LGBTQ+ Movement: Visibility Through Fashion

Fashion has always been a survival tool for the **queer community**.

In the early 20th century, LGBTQ+ people had to **hide in plain sight**, using clothing as a coded language to find each other. **A single red tie, a subtly positioned pinky ring, a well-placed piece of lavender**—these weren't just style choices; they were lifelines.

Then came the Stonewall riots in 1969, which sparked the modern LGBTQ+ rights movement. By the time the **Pride movement** emerged in the 1970s, queer fashion had evolved into something loud, proud, and impossible to ignore. **Rainbow flags, leather culture, drag, and gender-fluid fashion** became a direct challenge to the rigid norms of heterosexual society.

Fast forward to today, and **gender-neutral fashion** is having its moment. Harry Styles wears a dress on the cover of *Vogue*, Billy Porter redefines red carpet menswear, and Gen Z has largely rejected traditional gendered clothing altogether. But none of this happened in a vacuum—it's the result of **decades of LGBTQ+ defiance, where dressing outside the binary wasn't just a trend, but a fight for survival**.

Why Fashion Is Always Political (Even When You Think It's Not)

People love to dismiss fashion as **shallow, frivolous, apolitical**. But here's the truth:

- The ability to wear whatever you want? That's **privilege**.
- The fact that some people are punished for their clothing choices? That's **oppression**.
- The idea that fashion is *just* about aesthetics? That's **bullshit**.

From **hijabs to high heels, crop tops to combat boots**, what we wear is always communicating something. Sometimes that message is personal; other times, it's a full-scale revolution.

But make no mistake: **fashion is power**.

And as long as systems of oppression exist, people will keep using their clothing to fight back.

Because when words aren't enough, when laws are unjust, when society wants you to disappear—sometimes, the loudest thing you can do is **show up in an outfit that refuses to be ignored**.

The Politics of Hair – A Crown or a Constraint?

In 2019, a high school wrestler in New Jersey was forced to cut his dreadlocks *on the spot* before a match. The referee gave him a choice: chop them off or forfeit. The video of him standing there—humiliated, as his hair was hacked away—went viral, and suddenly, the world was reminded of something Black people already knew:

Hair is never just hair.

Across cultures, communities, and generations, **hair has been political**. It has been a tool of self-expression, a marker of identity, and, all too often, a battleground for control.

Who gets to wear their hair how they want? Whose hair is deemed "professional"? Whose hair is policed, and whose is praised? This chapter unpacks the racial, cultural, and gendered politics of hair—because whether it's an afro, a hijab, or a corporate-friendly bob, **what's on your head says more than you think**.

THE RACIAL POLITICS OF HAIR – Afros, Locs, and the Battle for Acceptance

Black hair has always been a site of resistance.

During slavery, Africans in America were often forced to **shave their heads** as a way to strip them of their identity and culture. Later, as racism codified itself into every aspect of American life, **European hair became the "gold standard"**, and Black people were pressured to conform.

- In the early 1900s, Black women were encouraged to **straighten their hair** to be considered "respectable."
- In the 1960s and '70s, the **Black Power movement reclaimed natural hair**, making afros a symbol of strength and defiance.
- Today, **corporate America still punishes Black hair**, with employees being told their locs, braids, and afros are "unprofessional."

The legal system hasn't helped. Until recently, **Black people could be fired for wearing their natural hair**. Schools have sent students home for having braids. Beauty pageants and modeling agencies have long favored straight-haired contestants. And while white celebrities like Kim Kardashian profit off of wearing cornrows or locs, Black people wearing the same styles are seen as *unruly* or *ghetto*.

The fact that Black people are still fighting for the right to wear their natural hair **without consequence** proves that beauty standards have never been neutral.

They've been built for—and by—those in power.

Hijabs, Headscarves, and the Fight Over Religious Expression

For Muslim women, hair politics take on a different—but equally controversial—dimension.

The hijab is one of the most misunderstood pieces of clothing in the world. In some places, it's a symbol of oppression; in others, it's a **deeply personal choice**. But no matter where you look,

women's hair—especially covered hair—seems to make people uncomfortable.

• In **France**, hijabs are banned in schools and government jobs.

• In **Iran**, women are forced by law to cover their hair, and many are arrested for refusing.

• In **India**, Muslim students have been **barred from classrooms** for wearing hijabs.

The message is clear: when women wear hijabs by choice, they're seen as oppressed. When they fight to remove them, they're seen as radical. Either way, **their bodies remain sites of control and debate**.

At the heart of this issue is a **larger question about autonomy**: Who gets to decide what a woman wears? Who decides what's appropriate, professional, or acceptable? And why do people feel entitled to control women's bodies—right down to the strands of their hair?

Why "Professional" = Whitewashed

Let's talk about the **unspoken rules of corporate grooming**.

For decades, corporate America has operated on **Eurocentric beauty standards**. Straight, neatly styled hair is considered "clean-cut," while afros, braids, and locs are labeled "distracting."

Consider these examples:
- **In 2010, BP Oil fired a Black woman for wearing locs**, claiming her hairstyle violated their dress code.
- **In 2017, a U.S. court ruled that companies could legally refuse to hire someone because of their dreadlocks**.
- **Black women spend 9x more on haircare than white women**—not because they want to, but because the pressure to conform is baked into the system.

It's no accident that "acceptable" hairstyles **just so happen** to align with Eurocentric beauty standards. The expectation that Black and brown people must alter their natural hair for work is a form of **racial gatekeeping**—one that reinforces who belongs in professional spaces and who doesn't.

But the tide is turning.

In recent years, the **CROWN Act** (Creating a Respectful and Open World for Natural Hair) has been gaining momentum. Passed in states like California and New York, it bans discrimination against natural hair in schools and workplaces. It's a small—but significant—step toward **dismantling the racist beauty hierarchy**.

The Billion-Dollar Hair Industry: Who Profits?

The hair industry is worth over **$87 billion**, and no group spends more on haircare than Black women.

But here's the irony: despite **Black consumers driving the market**, the industry is **dominated by non-Black ownership**.

- Many of the biggest beauty brands making money from relaxers, wigs, and hair extensions are **owned by white corporations**.
- Korean-owned beauty supply stores **control the distribution of Black haircare products**, often shutting out Black entrepreneurs.
- Meanwhile, Black hairstylists face hurdles in the **cosmetology industry**, where licensing laws often favor Eurocentric hair techniques.

The commercialization of Black hair isn't new. **Madam C.J. Walker**, the first Black female millionaire, built her empire on haircare products for Black women. But today, the industry has become **less about empowering Black consumers and more about profiting off their insecurities**.

Personal Reflection: A Hairstyle That Changed How I Was Perceived

Hair is personal. And for many of us, **changing our hair has changed our lives**.

For me, it was the time I chopped my long, "safe" hair into a short, edgy cut. Suddenly, I was treated differently. People assumed I was bolder, more opinionated, more rebellious.

For others, it's when they **embrace their natural curls after years of straightening**. Or when they wear their **first hijab in public**. Or when they **shave their head entirely, rejecting femininity altogether**.

We all have a hair story. And whether we realize it or not, our hair is constantly sending messages—to the world, and to ourselves.

Conclusion: Reclaiming the Power of Hair

Hair has been used to **control, police, and define us** for centuries. But it has also been a tool of **resistance, empowerment, and self-expression**.

- **For Black people**, reclaiming natural hair is an act of defiance.
- **For women in hijabs**, wearing it by choice is a form of autonomy.
- **For anyone challenging gender norms**, breaking traditional hair expectations is liberation.

At the end of the day, the goal isn't just about **being allowed to wear our hair however we want**. The goal is to **live in a world where our hair doesn't define our worth in the first place**.

Because whether we wear it straight or curly, short or long, covered or free—the real power lies in **owning the choice**.

High Heels, Lipstick, and Feminism – Empowerment or Oppression?

Are We Dressing for Ourselves or for the Patriarchy?
A bold red lip. A stiletto heel. A corset cinched so tight it could make a Victorian woman faint.

For centuries, beauty and femininity have walked a fine line between **empowerment and oppression**. On one hand, makeup, heels, and traditionally "feminine" fashion have been used to control and constrain women. On the other, reclaiming these aesthetics has been a radical act—turning tools of subjugation into weapons of power.

So, which is it?

Is wearing high heels an act of submission or defiance? Does loving fashion make you complicit in patriarchal beauty standards, or does it allow you to redefine them? And more importantly—can we *ever* separate personal choice from societal conditioning?

The answer isn't simple. But in this chapter, we're going to try to untangle it.

. . .

The High Heel Dilemma – A Symbol of Power or Pain?

There's nothing quite like the *click, click, click* of high heels on a polished floor. It's a sound that commands attention, a sound that says: **I have arrived.**

But let's not forget what heels actually *do*.

• They force women to walk in an unnatural, submissive posture—hips swaying, balance precarious.

• They're literally **painful**. A study found that **71% of women who wear high heels experience foot problems** like bunions and nerve damage.

• They've historically been used to **limit mobility**. It's hard to run, to fight, to move freely when your shoes are designed to slow you down.

And yet—women still wear them. Not just because society expects it, but because *we like them*. Because they make us feel taller, sexier, more powerful. And that's where the contradiction lies.

Even in professional settings, heels have been **enforced as part of dress codes**. In 2016, a London receptionist was **sent home from work for refusing to wear heels**, sparking global outrage. Meanwhile, male CEOs walk around in comfortable loafers while female executives teeter in stilettos. So if heels are really about *power*, why are they still *required* for women but not for men?

At the same time, some women—especially in male-dominated fields—use heels as **armor**. A towering stiletto can be a psychological weapon, a visual statement of dominance. **If I have to play this game, I might as well play to win.**

So, are heels a tool of oppression or a tool of power? The answer depends on who's wearing them—and why.

Lipstick, Corsets, and the Feminist Paradox

Lipstick has a long and complicated history.

• In **ancient Egypt**, Cleopatra used crushed bugs to stain her lips red.

- In **medieval Europe**, red lips were considered sinful—because, of course, women weren't allowed to be *too*attractive.
- By the **20th century**, red lipstick became a symbol of rebellion—worn by suffragettes in protest against gender norms.

Today, the debate still rages on. Is makeup an oppressive beauty standard, forcing women to present themselves as flawless at all times? Or is it an art form, a tool of self-expression?

Then there's the corset.

Once a literal cage for women's bodies—squeezing ribs, restricting movement, and causing fainting spells—the corset was a symbol of **female restriction** for centuries. Then, in the 21st century, it made a comeback—not as a necessity, but as **a fashion statement**.

Kim Kardashian wore a modern corset so tight at the Met Gala that she **reportedly couldn't sit down or breathe properly**. Meanwhile, Gen Z has adopted corsets as a *feminist* fashion trend, reclaiming them as a symbol of sexual and bodily autonomy.

The same piece of clothing that once **imprisoned women** is now being worn by choice. So does that make it feminist?

Or does it just prove that the patriarchy is good at repackaging oppression as empowerment?

THE FOURTH-WAVE FEMINIST AESTHETIC – Can We Reclaim Femininity?

Once upon a time, feminism meant burning bras and rejecting beauty norms. But **fourth-wave feminism** (aka the feminism of the social media era) is less about rejecting femininity and more about **redefining it**.

This is the era of the **bimbo resurgence**, the **Barbie-core movement**, and the idea that embracing hyper-femininity can actually be an act of rebellion.

- The "bimbo" stereotype was once used to dismiss women—but modern bimbos like Paris Hilton and Megan Thee Stallion have

reclaimed it, proving that you can be both **glamorous and intelligent**.
- The **Barbie movie (2023)** flipped the script on traditional femininity, making pink, heels, and glitter into a feminist statement.
- Celebrities like **Lana Del Rey and Doja Cat** have embraced a "hyper-feminine, but self-aware" aesthetic—leaning into beauty standards while also critiquing them.

The message is clear: **being feminine isn't the problem. Being forced to be feminine is.**

When women choose to wear heels, lipstick, and body-hugging clothes *on their own terms*, it challenges the idea that femininity is *only* for male consumption.

But here's the real question—how much of our "choice" is actually **programming**?

The Illusion of "Personal Choice"

We love to believe that our choices are **entirely our own**. But can we *really* separate personal preference from **centuries of societal conditioning**?

Think about it:
- If beauty standards didn't exist, would we still feel the need to contour our cheekbones or pluck our eyebrows?
- If heels weren't associated with sex appeal and power, would we still wear them to job interviews?
- If society didn't reward youth and beauty, would we still spend thousands of dollars on anti-aging treatments?

It's easy to say, "I wear makeup for *me*," but do we? Or have we just **internalized the expectation** so deeply that it *feels* like personal choice?

This is the feminist paradox: **We don't want to be told what to do, but we also don't know if we ever really had a choice to begin with.**

. . .

CONCLUSION: So, Is It Empowerment or Oppression?

The answer is: **it's both.**

High heels can be a tool of oppression—but also a source of confidence.

Makeup can reinforce beauty standards—but also be a form of self-expression.

Fashion can restrict women—but also give them power.

The real issue isn't whether these things are *inherently* oppressive. It's **who controls the narrative**.

- If we wear heels because they make us feel powerful, **great**.
- If we wear lipstick because we love it, **amazing**.
- But if we feel pressured to conform just to be taken seriously? That's when the problem starts.

Ultimately, **true empowerment means choice without consequence**—and we're not there yet.

Until the day comes when a woman can walk into a boardroom in sneakers, skip the makeup, and still be treated with the same respect as a man in a suit, we'll keep having this debate.

Because in the end, the most radical thing a woman can wear isn't heels or red lipstick.

It's the freedom to decide *exactly* how she wants to present herself—without the world weighing in.

Part Three
The Future of Fashion – Where Do We Go From Here?

The Death of Trends – Will Fashion Ever Be Truly Inclusive?

Who Gets to Be "Fashionable"?
Once upon a time, fashion was dictated by a select few—designers in Paris, editors at *Vogue*, and celebrities walking red carpets. Trends were unveiled on runways months in advance, trickling down to the masses in carefully curated waves.

Then, the internet happened.

Now, trends are born on TikTok, spread like wildfire, and die just as fast. Designers are no longer the gatekeepers—**social media users are**. And while this shift has democratized fashion, it has also exposed an uncomfortable truth: **fashion has never been made for everyone**.

For decades, the industry has marginalized **plus-size bodies, disabled individuals, gender-nonconforming people, and anyone who doesn't fit the mold of "sample size, white, and conventionally attractive."** And while brands now tout "diversity" and "inclusivity" as selling points, how much of it is **real progress**—and how much is just a **marketing ploy**?

This chapter explores the push for true inclusivity in fashion, the rise of genderless clothing, and what happens when social media—not designers—decides what's in style.

Diversity in Fashion: Progress or Performance?

Let's state the obvious: **fashion has a diversity problem.**

For most of its history, the industry has been built on **exclusivity**—clothing made for the thin, the wealthy, the white. And while brands today slap "inclusive" onto their campaigns, the reality is far more complicated.

Modeling and the Runway Shift

- In the early 2000s, runways were still **90% white, size 0-2, and nearly identical** in look.
- By the late 2010s, the industry saw a shift—more models of color, a handful of plus-size models, and the occasional person with a disability.
- But in 2022, **only 0.6% of runway models were plus-size**. And of those who were, most were still on the smaller end of the plus spectrum.

Meanwhile, mainstream brands love **diversity for the campaign but not for the clothes**. They'll showcase a size-20 model in an ad, but the largest size available? A 12.

Diversity sells. But does the industry really want to change?

The Rise of Genderless Fashion: Breaking the Binary or Just Another Trend?

For decades, fashion has been rigidly **gendered**. Pink for girls, blue for boys. Dresses for women, suits for men.

Then came **Gen Z**, a generation raised on the internet and largely uninterested in outdated gender norms. As a result, we're seeing the biggest shift in fashion since women started wearing pants.

- **Celebrities like Harry Styles, Lil Nas X, and Bad

Bunny are wearing skirts, nail polish, and traditionally "feminine" silhouettes—without apology.

- **Fashion houses like Gucci and Balenciaga** are launching genderless collections, blurring the lines between menswear and womenswear.
- **Retailers like Phluid Project and Telfar** are pioneering the gender-neutral shopping experience.

But here's the catch: **is fashion really becoming genderless, or is it just playing dress-up?**

Because while the industry celebrates *men* in skirts as "revolutionary," queer and trans people have been defying gender norms through fashion **long before it was trendy**—and they weren't applauded for it. In fact, they were (and still are) punished for it.

So is this a real shift, or just another **trend for cishet men to experiment with before moving on**?

What Happens When Social Media Drives Fashion Instead of Designers?

For most of fashion history, designers dictated trends. Now, **TikTok does.**

Fashion cycles that once lasted **years** now last **weeks**. Aesthetic trends—like cottagecore, Y2K, clean girl, and balletcore—rise and fall in record time. Microtrends are replacing traditional seasonal collections. And instead of designers setting the tone, it's **influencers, fast fashion brands, and algorithm-driven content creators**.

The result? A few things:

1 Trends move at breakneck speed, leading to mass overconsumption. (See: the Sheinification of fashion.)

2 Fashion feels increasingly... unoriginal. (When everyone dresses the same, personal style suffers.)

3 Designers are forced to react instead of create.

Instead of setting trends, they're now **following** them—often scrambling to keep up with TikTok.

And while social media has **made fashion more accessible**, it has also **flattened individuality**. If your entire wardrobe is dictated by what's "trending" on your feed, are you actually dressing for *you*—or for the algorithm?

PERSONAL STORY: The Moment I Realized Fashion Wasn't Made for Everyone

It hit me in a dressing room.

I was standing under the fluorescent lights, trying on a pair of designer jeans, the kind I had seen in every fashion magazine, the kind *cool girls* wore. I had imagined they would make me look effortless. Instead, I couldn't even pull them past my thighs.

The largest size in the store was a **10**. I was a **12**.

That was the moment I realized: **fashion was never made for everyone.**

It wasn't just about size. It was about **race, gender, disability, class**—about all the invisible barriers that decide who gets to participate in fashion and who doesn't.

Because even as brands claim to be "inclusive," the reality is still this:

- If you're plus-size, your options are **limited**.
- If you're disabled, finding fashionable clothes that work for you is **nearly impossible**.
- If you're not rich, keeping up with trends can feel like **a full-time job**.

Fashion *wants* to be inclusive. But inclusivity isn't about a **marketing campaign**—it's about **fundamentally changing the system**.

WILL Fashion Ever Be Truly Inclusive?

Maybe. But only if it moves beyond **token representation** and into **actual change**.

That means:

- **Expanding size ranges**—not just for show, but for real.
- **Normalizing disabled and trans bodies in fashion**—not as "diversity hires," but as part of the industry.
- **Breaking down the class barriers in fashion,**

making style accessible beyond just fast fashion or luxury brands.

Because **real fashion liberation isn't about keeping up with trends**—it's about **dismantling the idea that you have to fit a mold to belong**.

And if the future of fashion has any hope, it's in people who are tired of playing by the old rules.

People who are making their own.

FINAL THOUGHTS: The Death of Trends?

Fashion as we know it is changing. Trends are moving too fast to last. Designers no longer control what's in. And traditional ideas of "who fashion is for" are being torn down—piece by piece.

Maybe, in a way, **this is the death of trends as we know them.**

Because if fashion is going to have a future, it can't just be about **what's in style**.

It has to be about **who gets to participate in it**—and on whose terms.

And if the old system refuses to change?

Maybe it's time to burn it down and build something better.

The AI Stylist and the Metaverse Closet – The Digital Future of Fashion

What Happens When Your Clothes Are Just Data?

Imagine waking up, scrolling through your phone, and letting an **AI stylist** pick your outfit for the day. Not just any outfit—one that perfectly matches your mood, the weather, and the latest trends. No shopping required, no laundry to do. Your digital wardrobe is **limitless**—and so is your style.

Now imagine a world where **your most expensive outfit doesn't exist in real life**. It's an NFT, a designer dress made of pixels, worn by your avatar in the metaverse. It costs **thousands of dollars** but has no physical form.

Sounds futuristic? It's already happening.

The fashion industry is going through a **digital revolution**, and AI, virtual fashion, and the metaverse are rewriting the rules of style. But is this the future of self-expression—or just another way to commodify identity?

This chapter explores **how AI, NFTs, and digital fashion are reshaping the industry**—and whether these new technologies will actually make fashion more inclusive or just **recreate old biases in a new world**.

AI STYLISTS: The Death of Personal Style or the Ultimate Convenience?

Picture this: You stand in front of a smart mirror. It scans your body, analyzes your past fashion choices, and suggests **the perfect outfit**. Not just something that looks good—but something that takes into account your body shape, skin tone, and personal preferences.

This is the promise of **AI styling**, and it's already creeping into everyday life.

• **Apps like Cladwell and The Yes** use AI to build personalized wardrobes.

• **Zalando and Amazon's AI stylists** analyze your past purchases to predict what you'll want next.

• **Meta's AI fashion research** is training computers to understand and recommend fashion based on images and data.

On one hand, AI could **make fashion more accessible**—helping people discover styles that truly work for them, eliminating sizing struggles, and reducing the **waste of fast fashion**.

On the other, **there's a dark side**:

1 AI thrives on data, and fashion is deeply personal. If an algorithm dictates what we wear, do we lose individuality?

2 Tech companies will control what's "trendy." If AI is deciding what's stylish, do we just become **slaves to an algorithm**?

3 It could reinforce existing beauty standards. AI is only as smart as its programming, and if that programming is biased (which it often is), it could **exclude marginalized bodies**—just like traditional fashion has for decades.

AI fashion sounds like the future, but we have to ask: **do we really want computers making style decisions for us?**

. . .

THE RISE OF VIRTUAL FASHION – Owning Clothes You Can't Wear

Why buy **physical** clothes when you can buy **digital** ones?

Sounds ridiculous—until you realize people are already **spending thousands on digital fashion.**

• **Gucci sold a virtual handbag for $4,115**—more than the cost of the physical version.

• **Nike acquired RTFKT, a digital sneaker company**, proving that virtual kicks are a serious business.

• **Balenciaga partnered with Fortnite**, selling skins (aka digital outfits) that cost as much as real clothes.

The logic is simple: **We spend so much time online, why wouldn't we want our avatars to look as good as we do in real life?**

For gamers, influencers, and metaverse enthusiasts, digital fashion isn't just a gimmick—it's a **new status symbol**. Instead of flexing a designer bag on Instagram, you can flex it in a virtual world.

And there are some upsides:

• **Sustainability** – No waste, no textile pollution.

• **Endless creativity** – Designers can create **gravity-defying, futuristic** outfits that would be impossible in real life.

• **Accessibility** – People who can't afford luxury in real life might own digital versions.

But here's the question: **If digital fashion becomes the future, does it make real-world fashion irrelevant?**

Or worse—does it create **a new kind of exclusivity**, where only those who can afford the **most expensive pixels** are seen as fashionable?

NFTs AND FASHION – The Ultimate Status Symbol or Just Hype?

Let's talk about NFTs (Non-Fungible Tokens) in fashion.

An NFT is essentially a **digital certificate of ownership**—and fashion brands are jumping on the trend.

• **Dolce & Gabbana sold an NFT collection for $6 million.**

• **Nike has patented NFT sneakers, which exist only online.**

• **Adidas partnered with Bored Ape Yacht Club to release NFT streetwear.**

The idea? **Fashion isn't just about clothing—it's about owning a piece of culture.**

But here's the problem:

1 NFTs are still a bubble. Most people don't understand them, and those who do are mostly tech bros trying to make money.

2 They don't solve fashion's real issues. NFT fashion doesn't make **sizing more inclusive, representation better, or trends more sustainable**—it just makes fashion more digital.

3 They create another form of elitism. If traditional luxury fashion was about **who could afford the most expensive physical items**, NFT fashion is about **who can afford the most expensive pixels.**

So while NFT fashion might be the future, it's worth asking: **Is it a future where fashion becomes more democratic—or even more exclusive?**

THE DARK SIDE: Will the Metaverse Reinforce Real-World Biases?

The metaverse promises a world where **anyone can be anything**. No gender restrictions, no body shaming, no class barriers.

But let's be real—**biases don't just disappear when we go digital.**

1 Beauty standards still exist online. Even in virtual

worlds, avatars still conform to **Eurocentric beauty norms—thin, symmetrical, conventionally attractive**.

2 High-fashion metaverse spaces will still be for the elite. If luxury brands are already selling NFT clothes for thousands, how is that any different from **the real-world class divide?**

3 Fast fashion will still exist—but in a new way. Instead of mass-producing clothes, brands will **mass-produce digital skins**—creating the same **endless cycle of overconsumption** that real-world fast fashion does.

So while the metaverse *could* revolutionize fashion, we have to ask: **Are we actually building something new, or just recreating the same old problems in a virtual space?**

The Future: Will Fashion Be More Free or More Controlled?

So where do we go from here?

- **Will AI make fashion easier—or erase individuality?**
- **Will digital fashion be sustainable—or just another way to sell us more?**
- **Will the metaverse allow for self-expression—or just recreate the beauty hierarchy in a new form?**

The truth is, **fashion is entering a new era**, and no one really knows what it will look like yet.

But if history has taught us anything, it's this:

Fashion has always been about **identity, power, and access.**

And if the digital revolution doesn't address the real-world issues of **representation, inclusivity, and accessibility**—then it's not really progress. It's just another trend.

. . .

FINAL THOUGHTS: Do We Even Need Physical Clothes Anymore?

The idea of owning **nothing but digital clothes** sounds absurd now. But then again, so did the idea of **shopping entirely online** 20 years ago.

One thing is certain: **the way we engage with fashion is changing**—whether we like it or not.

The question is: **Will we control fashion's future, or will it control us?**

Because whether in the real world or the digital one, **fashion is still power.**

And we need to decide **who gets to wield it.**

The Case for Wearing Whatever the Hell You Want

What Happens When You Stop Caring About the Rules?

There's a moment of liberation that comes when you stop dressing for **them**—for the trend cycle, for the male gaze, for the unwritten rules of what's "acceptable" in society. It's the moment you step out in an outfit that feels *entirely* like you, knowing full well it might raise some eyebrows, but not giving a damn.

Maybe it's wearing a crop top even though some outdated beauty standard says you shouldn't.

Maybe it's ditching the high heels that once felt like a requirement.

Maybe it's embracing maximalism in a world that tells you to be polished and understated.

Maybe it's rejecting fashion altogether and deciding that your identity has nothing to do with what you put on your body.

Whatever it looks like, **true fashion liberation** isn't about following trends or rebelling against them. It's about stepping outside the system and saying, *I wear what I want, because I want to. Full stop.*

But getting to that point isn't easy.

We live in a world that constantly tells us **how to dress, how to present ourselves, how to be perceived**. The fashion industry is built on the idea that we must **keep up, buy more, and never feel completely satisfied**. And even the movements that claim to be about self-expression—whether it's high fashion, minimalism, or gender-neutral clothing—still carry **rules and expectations**.

So how do we actually *get free*?

This chapter is about **letting go of trends, gender norms, and external validation** to reclaim style as something deeply personal, deeply political, and deeply yours.

Why We're Taught to Obsess Over Fashion (Even When We Pretend We Don't)

Even if you think you don't care about fashion, fashion cares about you.

Society has always used clothing as a **shortcut for judgment**. It's how we decide:

- Who belongs and who doesn't.
- Who deserves respect and who doesn't.
- Who has power and who doesn't.

From the moment we're born, we're taught that **appearance equals value**. That our clothes aren't just clothes—they're a reflection of how smart, successful, or worthy we are.

Think about it:

- **Women are expected to look "polished"** at all times, because looking *too* comfortable = lazy.
- **Men are expected to stick to safe, neutral styles**, because too much self-expression = unserious.
- **Plus-size people are expected to "flatter" their bodies**, as if dressing for their own joy isn't an option.

- **Queer and gender-nonconforming people are often policed or even physically threatened** just for wearing what feels right to them.

Even in spaces that claim to be **progressive**, there's still an underlying pressure to present a certain way. Even "not caring" about fashion is, in itself, a **fashion choice**—one that often signals privilege.

Because the reality is, **not everyone gets to dress however the hell they want without consequences**.

Fashion as a Political Statement (Even When It's Not Meant to Be)

Clothing has always been political.
- The **Black Panthers** wore leather jackets and berets as a uniform of power.
- **Feminists** wore pantsuits to challenge male-dominated spaces.
- **LGBTQ+ activists** have used androgynous and flamboyant fashion to reclaim space.
- **Muslim women who choose to wear hijabs in Western countries** are often making a statement—even if they're just wearing what feels natural to them.

But here's the twist: **sometimes, the most radical thing you can do is wear what makes you happy.**
- If you're a woman who's spent years feeling like you *have* to be feminine, cutting your hair short and wearing baggy clothes might feel like a revolution.
- If you're a man who's spent years being told to "dress like a man," throwing on a skirt might feel like a protest.
- If you've spent your whole life chasing trends, stepping out of the cycle and wearing the same outfit on repeat might feel like rebellion.

Whatever it is, **fashion stops being a trap the moment you reclaim it on your own terms**.

The Lies We've Been Sold About "Personal Style"

We love the idea of "personal style." The notion that we all have an **innate** sense of fashion that's just waiting to be discovered.

But let's be real: **personal style isn't always personal.**

Most of the time, what we think of as "our style" has been influenced by **marketing, social norms, and the subconscious need for validation**. The "cool girl aesthetic," the "minimalist uniform," the "effortless streetwear look"—these are all *manufactured identities*, sold to us through social media and advertising.

So how do you know if your style is actually *yours*?

Start by asking:

1 Would I still wear this if nobody else saw me in it?

2 Am I dressing for my comfort, my joy, or someone else's approval?

3 Does this outfit feel like an extension of me—or just a costume I put on to fit in?

The goal isn't to burn your entire wardrobe and start over (unless you want to). It's about **making intentional choices that serve YOU, not the system**.

True Fashion Liberation = Wearing What You Want, Not What's Expected

What would happen if you woke up tomorrow and **stopped thinking about what's "flattering," "appropriate," or "on-trend"?**

What if you let go of:
- The need to dress a certain way to be "taken seriously"?
- The fear of wearing something "too much" or "too little"?
- The anxiety of being "overdressed" or "underdressed"?

The truth is, the fashion industry **needs us to be insecure** to keep making money.

It needs us to feel like we're *always* a few purchases away from finally getting it right.

But what if you already had it right?

What if you already *looked amazing*, just by dressing for **yourself?**

Final Thoughts: The Real Power of Fashion

Fashion is power.

Not because of **what you wear**, but because of **why you wear it**.

- If you wear heels, wear them because you *want to*, not because you *have to*.
- If you wear a suit, wear it because it makes you feel strong, not because society says it's the only way to be respected.
- If you wear sweatpants every day, do it because it makes you happy—not because you're hiding from self-expression.

At the end of the day, the most radical, liberating thing you can do is wear what makes you feel **like yourself**.

Because once you stop dressing for external validation, once you break free from the fashion-industrial complex that tells you what you *should* wear, you realize:

The best thing you can put on is confidence.

And *that* never goes out of style.

The Final Argument: Fashion Is Power—Use It Wisely.

So here's the takeaway:

You don't have to follow trends.

You don't have to rebel against them, either.

You don't have to dress for men, for women, for society, for Instagram, or for anyone other than *yourself*.

Because when fashion stops being a trap and starts being a tool, it becomes exactly what it was always meant to be: **a way to tell the world exactly who you are—on your own terms.**

And if anyone doesn't like it?

That's their problem. Not yours.

Conclusion: Fashion as a Tool, Not a Trap

Fashion is a paradox. It is both **creative expression and capitalist machine**, both **liberation and limitation**, both **deeply personal and entirely political**.

It allows us to tell the world who we are—yet it also dictates who gets to belong.

It can be a means of self-empowerment—but it's also been used to control, suppress, and exclude.

It encourages individuality—yet it thrives on conformity.

And perhaps most frustratingly, even when we *think* we're opting out, we're still playing the game.

For centuries, we've been taught that fashion is either **frivolous or all-important**—that caring about it too much makes you shallow, but caring too little makes you invisible. We are told to "be ourselves" while being bombarded with messages about what that *should* look like. Even our rejection of trends becomes its own trend.

So where does that leave us?

It leaves us at a crossroads.

The Tension: Fashion as Freedom vs. Fashion as Control

Conclusion: Fashion as a Tool, Not a Trap

The truth is, fashion is neither inherently oppressive nor inherently liberating—it is simply **a tool**.

Like any tool, it can be wielded in different ways. It can be used to **uplift or destroy**, to **break barriers or reinforce them**, to **create joy or manufacture insecurity**. The problem isn't fashion itself—it's **who controls it, who profits from it, and who gets left out of the conversation**.

- **When fashion is about self-expression, it's freeing.**
- **When fashion is about approval, it's exhausting.**
- **When fashion is about creativity, it's revolutionary.**
- **When fashion is about control, it's dangerous.**

And most of the time? **It's all of those things at once.**

A Call to Rethink Our Relationship with Style

So how do we navigate this? How do we engage with fashion without letting it own us?

The answer isn't to reject fashion altogether. It's to **engage with it consciously**—to recognize that every purchase, every trend, every choice exists within a larger system.

This doesn't mean we should feel **guilty** for loving fashion. It means we should feel **aware**.

- Aware of where our clothes come from.
- Aware of why we're drawn to certain styles.
- Aware of the messages we send with what we wear—and the ones that are projected onto us.

We can love fashion while questioning it.

We can participate in trends while understanding their lifecycle.

We can enjoy style while knowing that what we wear is shaped by forces bigger than us.

The Final Takeaway: Fashion is a Reflection of the World We Live In

Fashion doesn't exist in a vacuum.

It reflects **power structures, social movements, economic systems, and cultural shifts**. It reveals what a

Conclusion: Fashion as a Tool, Not a Trap

society values—and what it suppresses. It tells a story about **who holds influence, who is seen, and who is erased**.

And most importantly, **fashion is never just about fabric—it's about identity.**

So as we move forward, the challenge isn't to abandon fashion. It's to reclaim it. To use it on **our** terms. To recognize that, at its best, fashion is a tool—a way to define ourselves in a world that is constantly trying to define us first.

Because in the end, the most powerful thing we can do isn't just to wear whatever we want.

It's to know exactly **why** we're wearing it.

And that? That's real fashion freedom.